Multiple Intelligences & After-School Environments

Keeping ALL Children in Mind

by David L. Whitaker

Logical/Mathematical

Linguistic

Intrapersonal

Musical

Spatial

Interpersonal

Naturalist

Body/Kinesthetic

School-Age NOTES • Nashville, TN

David L. Whitaker has worked in child care since 1987 as lead teacher, program coordinator, trainer and consultant. He has worked with all ages of children in a variety of program settings including preschool, kindergarten, before-and-after school programs and summer programs. In 1998 David formed Toolbox Training in response to the increasing demand for tools by which to improve the quality of child care. He has developed over a dozen training packages which he uses in his workshops. Titles include *Discipline with Dignity* and *Connect with Parents: The K.I.D.S. Method*. David serves on the Missouri School-Age Care Coalition state board and has served on the Missouri Accreditation state board and the Greater Kansas City Association for the Education of Young Children. He has a Bachelor of Arts degree in Speech Communication and a Masters in Education. He currently lives in the Kansas City, MO area with his wife, Becky.

Other titles by **David L. Whitake**r include: *Games, Games, Games: Creating Hundreds of Group Games & Sports* and *In Pursuit of NSACA Accreditation*.

For more information on **Toolbox Training** and workshops by David Whitaker:

TOOLBOX TRAINING
P.O. Box 25565, Kansas City MO 64119
Phone: 816-455-0729
email: toolbox_training@yahoo.com
www.toolboxonline.bigstep.com

Cover Design: Denise Scott, Nashville, TN.

ISBN: 0-917505-12-3

Published by School-Age NOTES, P.O. Box 40205, Nashville TN 37204

TABLE OF CONTENTS

INTRODUCTION

Why I Wrote This Book

I started working in the school-age care (SAC) field in 1987. Like many of my co-workers, I stumbled into the profession. With a Bachelor's degree in speech communication, my intention was to go into training and consulting. I had not imagined myself overseeing art projects and games of tag.

However, all things come full circle. I discovered the perfect blend of my profession that was and my profession that was to be. In 1998, I formed my own company - Toolbox Training - with the mission to deliver high-quality workshops, consultation, and resources to SAC and early childhood (EC) programs in urban, suburban, and rural environments.

I also decided it was time to return to school. If I was going to train adults on working with children, I wanted more expertise in the area myself. I opted for a Master's Degree in Curriculum and Instruction through the Creative Arts in Learning program of Lesley University's Graduate School of Arts and Social Sciences. (Whew! That's quite a mouthful!)

In any event, the Master's in Education program focused on meeting the needs of all learners through the use of creative arts. One such way was through understanding multiple intelligences (MI), a theory originally proposed by Howard Gardner in *Frames of Mind* (1983). Gardner suggests that traditional Western education reaches only a fraction of learners. The child who excels in readin', writin', and 'rithmetic goes to the head of the class. Less celebrated are the kids who draw best, run fastest, sing loudest, socialize most, have the keenest sense of self awareness, and just like collecting bugs on the playground.

On the flip side, SAC and EC environments have long celebrated children's abilities and strengths through activities and interest centers devoted to the likes of art, music, and dramatic play. However, this focus on play leads many people to assume that child care is just "babysitting."

This book will help professionals working in either school or child care settings to meet all learners' needs by infusing classroom staples (e.g., reading, writing, math, science) and the arts (e.g., visual art, music, drama, creative movement).

The first part of this book offers an overview of Gardner's Multiple Intelligence theory and its implications for classrooms and child care programs.

The second part analyzes the intelligences in more detail. A definition of each intelligence is accompanied by a profile of characteristics that might fit someone with this intelligence. In addition, each intelligence is accompanied by suggested activities, materials, and areas in which to organize those materials.

The final section focuses on interest centers that support the co-existence of the arts alongside the basics. Interest centers (or areas) are not aligned with specific intelligences. The world doesn't work that way, so neither should the environments in which children learn. That means, for example, that an art area is not exclusive to the child with spatial intelligence. A body/kinesthetic child might be kneading dough; a child with naturalist intelligence might be doing leaf rubbings.

Of course, no child's intelligence is exclusive either. Even a child with an exceptional amount of musical intelligence will explore other interests. Any learning environment should offer children chances to explore all of the intelligences.

While the approaches may differ, classrooms and child care programs are committed to the betterment of the child. This book is written from a child care perspective, but with the idea that any professionals who work with children will benefit from the content. After all, what do any of us need to succeed? We need caring people in a caring environment who care most about letting us find out who we are. It would be a crime not to acknowledge children with a gift for gab, knack for doodling, or proclivity toward snagging whatever six-legged critters crawl their way.

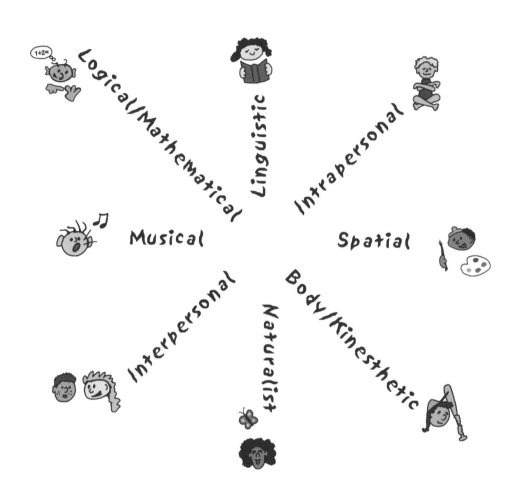

Multiple Intelligences & After-School Environments

Multiple Intelligences

NOTES

MULTIPLE INTELLIGENCES

What Are They?

The theory of multiple intelligences (MI) was developed in 1983 by Dr. Howard Gardner, professor of education at Harvard University. It suggests that the traditional notion of intelligence, based on I.Q. testing, is far too limited. He defined intelligence as the "ability to solve problems, or to fashion products, that are valued in one or more cultural or community settings" (Gardner, 1993, p.7). Initially Gardner's MI theory accounted for seven intelligences (Gardner, 1983) to better indicate the range of human potential in children and adults. These intelligences are:

 Linguistic (word smart)

 Logical/Mathematical (number/reasoning smart)

 Spatial (picture smart)

 Body/Kinesthetic (body smart)

 Musical (music smart)

 Interpersonal (people smart)

 Intrapersonal (self smart)

He later suggested an eighth:

 Naturalist (nature smart)

(Terms "word smart" "nature smart," etc. from Armstrong, 1999 - Table of Contents)

There's even been some consideration of a ninth intelligence — existential intelligence (Armstrong, 1999)— but this book will not cover that one.

MULTIPLE INTELLIGENCES

Criteria

Some critics would suggest that Gardner's MI theory must not be particularly sound if an eighth and possibly ninth, intelligence have been added since his initial hypothesis. However, as Gardner himself says, "There is not, and there never can be, a single irrefutable and universally accepted list of human intelligences. There will never be a master list of three, seven, or three hundred intelligences which can be endorsed by all investigators." (Gardner, 1983, p.60)

Gardner does, however, detail criteria for determining intelligences:

1. **Vulnerability to impairment through injury** - when one suffers a stroke or other kind of brain damage, can this intelligence be spared or destroyed? (Gardner, 1993, p.7)

2. **The existence of special populations** - are there people such as the learning disabled, idiot savants, prodigies, and autistics, with specialized abilities in this area? (Gardner, 1993, p.8)

3. **An identifiable set of operations** - does this intelligence have separate cognitive processes in areas of memory, attention, perception, and problem solving? For example, one may have a better memory for something musical than something linguistic (Armstrong, 1999, p.16).

4. **A developmental history** - does this intelligence emerge at a certain point in childhood and have future potential for growth, followed by a decline as the person ages? (Armstrong, 1999, p.14)

5. **An evolutionary history** - can this intelligence be traced back through time? Is it rooted in biology; i.e. can it be observed in animals? Example: birds have musical abilities and interpersonal intelligence is suggested by animals moving in herds.

6. **Support from psychological experiments** - can tests be performed to show that tasks demonstrating different intelligences will interfere with one another? Will these tasks transfer across different contexts? Example: a person with a great ear for musical pitch might be unable to determine the difference between "th" and "sh" as verbal sounds (Armstrong, 1999, p.16).

7. **Support from testing** - can standard tests be performed that will show evidence of this intelligence? Gardner criticizes I.Q. tests for only showing evidence of linguistic and logical/mathematical intelligence. Other tests can explore one's abilities in the other intelligences.

8. **Capable of being symbolized** - can ideas and experiences be expressed through representations of this intelligence? Examples include alphabets for linguistic intelligence, numbers for logical/mathematical, musical notes for musicians, gestures for body/kinesthetic, social symbols like waving goodbye for interpersonal (Armstrong, 1999, p. 13).

(Criteria originally outlined by Gardner, 1983, pp.62-69.)

Implications to Schools

Schools exist to provide children with tools necessary to conduct their lives and then formally assess children's abilities. Unfortunately, the American education system suffers from what Howard Gardner calls the "Westist, Testist, Bestist Syndrome." In other words, our system is biased toward Western culture, focuses heavily on testing, and celebrates those who perform the best according to linguistic and logical/mathematical intelligences (1993, p.12).

Gardner says that we should give equal attention to artists, architects, musicians, naturalists, designers, dancers, therapists, entrepreneurs, and others who enrich the world in which we live (www.thomasarmstrong.com). Children with these gifts are generally not celebrated in school. In fact, they are often labeled "learning disabled," "ADD" (attention deficit disorder) or "underachievers" (www.thomasarmstrong.com).

Gardner states that a school should prepare children for vocations appropriate to their intelligences (Gardner, 1993, p.9). In other words, along with core instructional content, children should receive assessment of their intelligences and opportunities to explore those intelligences.

The task is not an impossibility in the school environment. Bruce Campbell developed a program to teach to the intelligences in his third grade classroom. Approximately two and a half hours of each school day are devoted to students working in centers. Students move in groups of three and four through all the centers spending about twenty minutes at each one. For example, while studying a unit on Planet Earth, the centers provided activities to help the students learn about the structure of the earth (Campbell, 1999). The centers and activities for all but the naturalist intelligences included:

Multiple Intelligences & After-School Environments

Reading Center (*linguistic*) - students read *The Magic School Bus*, which depicted a group of school children exploring the inside of the earth (Campbell, 1999).

Math Center (*logical/mathematical*) - each group worked with geometric concepts of concentric circles, radius, diameter, etc. (Campbell, 1999)

Art Center (*spatial*) - children cut out concentric circles of different sizes and colors, pasting and labeling them to identify the different zones (Campbell, 1999).

Building Center (*body/kinesthetic*) - students constructed three-layer replicas of the earth with three colors of clay to represent the core, the mantle and the crust. They sliced their clay earths in half for a cross-section view (Campbell, 1999).

Music Center (*musical*) - a listening/spelling activity. Students listened to music while studying spelling words such as earth, crust, mantle and core (Campbell, 1999).

Working Together Center (*interpersonal*) - children engaged in a cooperative learning activity where they had to read a fact sheet on the earth and jointly answer questions (Campbell, 1999).

Personal Work Center (*intrapersonal*) - children did a fantasy writing activity on the subject: "Things you would take with you on a journey to the center of the earth" (Campbell, 1999).

One doesn't have to teach or learn something in all eight ways. Just see what the possibilities are and decide which particular pathways interest you the most or seem to be the most effective teaching or learning tools. The theory of MI is so intriguing because it expands our horizon of available teaching and learning tools beyond the conventional linguistic and logical methods used in most schools (e.g. lecture, textbooks, writing assignments, formulas, etc.) (www.thomasarmstrong.com).

Implications to Child Care

The objectives of schools and child care programs are ultimately the same — provide children with the skills and tools necessary to conduct their lives. However, schools and child care programs approach these goals from very different sides.

The child care setting, whether it be a school-age program or an early childhood program, is well suited to providing children with opportunities to flourish in multiple areas. Child care programs have the luxury of letting children explore those intelligences for themselves. Child care also focuses on providing children with tools necessary to conduct their lives, but does so much more informally. Quality child care programs focus on providing children with choice, therefore letting them self-select activities that will reflect their intelligences.

Another advantage of the child care setting is that children can engage in activities that may not be within their "intelligence comfort zone." The child who may not have tapped into his spatial intelligence can experiment with art projects without risk of failure or poor assessment. There is no pressure to perform or pass a test.

Consequently, a child care program with a strong understanding and implementation of MI can offer children well-rounded opportunities that will meet all their needs.

The
Intelligences

THE INTELLIGENCES

An Introduction

In this section, you will meet children representing each of the eight intelligences.

- *Luisa* - the linguistic child
- *Max* - the logical/mathematical child
- *Stephon* - the spatial child
- *Becca* - the body/kinesthetic child
- *Mario* - the musical child
- *Ian* and *Ida* - the interpersonal children
- *Ira* - the intrapersonal child
- *Nayah* - the naturalist child

Definition: Each intelligence is first introduced with a "definition" page that describes the interests and abilities of children with this intelligence. Potential career choices for such children are also indicated. Finally, a more formal definition of the intelligence appears in a box on the page.

A Profile: This is a checklist that lets you see at a glance what factors indicate if someone possesses this intelligence.

Putting It into Action: Finally, each intelligence is accompanied by recommendations of how to meet the needs of children with this intelligence in your child care program. A box at the end indicates what areas (detailed in the third section of this book) might capture the interest of children with this intelligence.

LINGUISTIC INTELLIGENCE

Definition

 Luisa is quite the bookworm. She could read before she was in kindergarten and has buried her nose in books ever since. Of course, it has paid off for her in school. Since the traditional Western education system focuses so heavily on language, both written and oral, then she is at a distinct advantage in the classroom.

When Luisa isn't reading, she relishes any opportunity to talk with other kids. She loves to share with the group at gathering time. She might share a story or tell a joke or even recite a poem that she memorized.

Of course, Luisa's no slouch at writing either. If she isn't reading a story or telling a story, then she's probably writing one. She especially enjoys writing silly stories that are full of rhymes and puns and riddles.

Luisa has a gift for language. Because of her linguistic intelligence, she is fascinated with words, whether it be through reading, writing, speaking, or listening.

> *Linguistic intelligence is the ability to absorb information and communicate through reading, writing, speaking, and listening.*

When she grows up, Luisa might use her linguistic ability to be an author, storyteller, poet, playwright, orator, editor, journalist, trainer, or politician.

LINGUISTIC INTELLIGENCE

A Profile

How do you identify someone, either child or adult, as being strong in this intelligence? See if a majority of these characteristics fit. This person:

❏ Considers books very important.

❏ Has many favorite books.

❏ Was an early reader.

❏ Liked poems or stories even at a young age.

❏ Has an easy time memorizing stories, poems, historical facts, or other tidbits of information.

❏ Is entertained by tongue twisters, nonsense rhymes, or puns.

❏ Enjoys word games like *Scrabble*™, *Anagrams*, or *Password*™.

❏ Loves to look things up in the encyclopedia or dictionary.

❏ Has an easier time with English, social studies, and history than math and science.

❏ Has written something recently that he/she is particularly proud of or that earned recognition.

❏ Pays more attention to billboards than scenery when driving down the highway.

❏ Is very talkative.

❏ Spoke at an early age.

❏ Hears words in his/her head before reading, speaking, or writing them.

❏ Has to sometimes explain meanings of words to others that he/she used in writing and speaking.

❏ Frequently references things he/she has read or heard.

❏ Gets more from listening to the radio or a spoken-word cassette than television or film.

This checklist is adapted from materials created by Armstrong (1999, pp. 150-1) and Phipps (1997, p.9).

LINGUISTIC INTELLIGENCE

Putting It into Action

Because she loves language in all forms, Luisa will respond to activities and materials that promote reading, writing, speaking, talking and listening. Adults can do the following to meet the needs of children like Luisa:

Promote reading:

● Provide reading material for children (*stories, poetry, biographies, magazines, jokes, riddles, nursery rhymes, reference*).
● Establish a comfortable space for reading (*pillows, bean bags, rocking chair*) that is away from louder activities. Use a shelf or other means to attractively display reading materials.
● Make copies of books written by the children, laminate the covers, and put the books out for other children to read.
● If possible, arrange to use the school library regularly.
● Provide word puzzle books (*crosswords, word searches*). Offer table games that promote reading (*Scrabble*™, *Boggle*™).
● Label materials and areas so that children "see" language.

Promote writing:

● Encourage creative writing (*stories, poems, or otherwise*).
● Provide materials to allow children to make own books (*variety of paper and writing instruments, pencil sharpeners, fastening materials like staples and yarn, decorating materials like stamp pads and stickers*).
● Let children make and keep journals (*folders, notebooks, lined paper*).
● Offer a variety of writing surfaces (*table, desk, laptop desk, clipboard*).
● Let children create a newspaper for your program.
● Use computers!
● Let kids write out frustrations when they have problems.

(More activity and material ideas on next page.)

Promote speaking and talking:

● Give children time for informal conversation.
● Have daily sharing and/or discussion time.
● Give children chances for performance (*creative dramatics, joke telling, rapping, reading, poetry, singing jingles*).
● Give children opportunities to explore humor (*jokes, tongue twisters, silly riddles, funny rhymes*).
● Let children tape any of above or simply record their own voices. They could also conduct interviews (*tape recorder, blank cassettes, microphone*).
● Involve children in brainstorming and planning activities.

Promote listening:

● Read to children.
● Make up stories with children.
● Have a "listening center" (*tape player, headphones*).
● Give children taped stories (*purchased or homemade*).
● Bring in guest speakers.

Areas

Here's where Luisa, and children like her, are most likely to find these activities and materials:

● language area
● reading area
● writing area
● bookmaking area

● computer area
● communications area
● drama area

LOGICAL/MATHEMATICAL INTELLIGENCE

Definition

Max has a gift for numbers and excels at scientific reasoning. Like Luisa (linguistic intelligence), he does well in school. He's a whiz on math and science questions on standardized multiple choice tests found so prevalently in the traditional Western education system.

Max loves to do experiments. When someone brought in a pineapple for the kids to see, he was eager to measure it, weigh it, and study it with a magnifying glass. He quickly started asking questions like "What if we do this to it?" or "I wonder how many pineapples would fit in this room?"

Max also thinks in patterns. For example, when given a box of buttons, he immediately started sorting and categorizing them (color, size, shape, number of holes in each button). Of course, he also started hypothesizing about the origins of the buttons. "This one," he'd say, "must be from a coat because it's bigger. This white one, though, is probably from a man's shirt because my dad has a shirt with buttons like this on it."

Max has an ability to mentally process logical problems and equations. He uses numbers and reasoning effectively, thinks in patterns, and has a natural inclination to ask "What if?" questions.

> *Logical/mathematical intelligence is the ability to use numbers and reasoning effectively.*

When he grows up, Max might be a scientist, accountant, computer programmer, statistician, or mathematician.

LOGICAL/MATHEMATICAL INTELLIGENCE

A Profile

Profile adapted from materials developed by Armstrong (1999, p. 151) and Phipps (1997, p. 9)

How do you identify someone, either child or adult, as being strong in this intelligence? See if a majority of these characteristics fit. This person:

❑ Responds well to math and science.

❑ Thinks in clear, abstract, wordless, imageless concepts.

❑ Enjoys counting (especially as a child).

❑ Can easily compute numbers in his/her head.

❑ Understands new math concepts quickly.

❑ Likes games or brain teasers that require logical thinking.

❑ Looks for patterns and regularities in the world (e.g., noticing every third step on the stairs had a notch on it).

❑ Believes almost everything has a rational explanation.

❑ Is interested in the latest scientific developments.

❑ Enjoys science materials such as chemistry sets.

❑ Is curious about how things work or why things in nature happen the way they do.

❑ Likes to set up "What if?" experiments (for example, "What if we add salt to the play dough mixture?")

❑ Likes experimenting with cause-and-effect while playing with blocks or other toys.

❑ Feels more comfortable when something has been measured, categorized, analyzed, or quantified in some way.

❑ Likes finding logical flaws in things people say and do at home and at work.

❑ Responds to children's shows like *Mr. Wizard* and *The Wild Kingdom*, which deal with science or nature themes, or the parts of *Mr. Rogers' Neighborhood*, *Sesame Street*, or *Captain Kangaroo* that involve numbers and science experiments.

LOGICAL/MATHEMATICAL INTELLIGENCE

Putting It into Action

Because he has a head for numbers and logic, Max will respond to activities and materials that promote numbers, classification, sequencing, patterning, problem solving, and experimentation. Adults can do the following to meet the needs of children like Max:

Promote numbers:

● Provide math-related tools for children (*calculator, abacas, protractor, compass, etc.*).

● Let children make math-related materials (*graphs, charts*).

● Provide tools for measuring (*cups, spoons, containers, scales, rulers, tape measures*).

● Encourage children's time awareness through materials and actions (*kitchen timers, sand timers, schedules, time lines*).

● Stick to a daily schedule and let children know verbally and in writing what time each activity starts.

● Offer number-oriented puzzles and games (*Dominoes, War*).

Promote classification, sequencing, and patterning:

● Provide matching games for children (*Concentration, Guess Who, Old Maid, Go Fish, Crazy Eights*).

● Offer manipulatives and collections that allow children to sort and classify items by size, shape, color, etc. (*beads, buttons*).

● Give children materials that promote patterning (*pegs and pegboards, cut-out shapes, pattern blocks*).

● Provide various-sized containers for sorting and classifying objects and liquids.

(*More activity and material ideas on next page.*)

Promote problem solving and experimentation:

● Offer chances for scientific experiments (*kits, books of possible projects*). *

● Do cooking projects that allow for children to mix and measure ingredients, as well as experiment.

● Give children materials for exploring and experimenting (*magnifying glasses, prisms, mirrors, tweezers*).

● Establish an area where children can experiment with various textures (*water, sand, macaroni*).

● Provide children with tools for experimenting with the textures (*cups, funnels, sifters, eye droppers, sand toys*).

● Allow children access to a computer if at all possible.

● Have paper and pencil activities that promote logical thinking (*logic puzzles, material for coding and deciphering*).

* Note to adults - you don't have to know the answers to do science! The point is that kids are looking for the answers.

Areas
Here's where Max, and other children like him, are most likely to find these materials and activities:

● math area

● science area

● discovery area

● texture area

● computer area

● manipulatives area

● game area

SPATIAL INTELLIGENCE

Definition

 Stephon always seems to have a pencil or paintbrush in hand. He has a strong sense of color, line, shape, form, and space. With that ability, he is able to transform what he sees into visual representations.

If he isn't drawing, he's building. He'll take a set of blocks and construct an entire model of his house. If you ask him what he's building, he'll launch into a detailed account. "Well, this is my bedroom over here. All the blocks are blue since that's my favorite color. The red blocks are the living room. Actually, my living room is bigger than this, but there weren't enough red blocks." You get the picture. Then again, with Stephon, you always get the picture.

Because of his spatial intelligence, Stephon relies heavily on his sense of sight. He visualizes the world around him and then creates visual representations based on those perceptions and interpretations.

> *Spatial intelligence is the ability to visualize and create representations of what one sees.*

When he grows up, Stephon might be an artist, sculptor, architect, interior decorator, engineer, inventor, map maker, or a sea captain. When asked about the last profession, he says, "I've never met a sea captain, but I put together this puzzle once and it had a picture of this sea captain and he had to sail by finding his way by the stars. I think I'd be good at that."

SPATIAL INTELLIGENCE

A Profile

How do you identify someone, either child or adult, as being strong in this intelligence? See if a majority of these characteristics fit. This person:

❑ Enjoys drawing and painting.

❑ Passes time doodling.

❑ Responds well to color.

❑ Visualizes things in his/her head that are almost as real as objects in real life.

❑ Can easily imagine how something might appear if it were observed from a bird's-eye view.

❑ Has vivid and colorful visual dreams.

❑ Prefers heavily-illustrated reading material.

❑ Frequently uses a camera or camcorder.

❑ Enjoys jigsaw puzzles, mazes, and other visual puzzles.

❑ Is better at geometry than algebra.

❑ Likes taking things apart and putting things together (e.g., toys, simple machines, and/or puzzles).

❑ Plays with erector sets, Tinker Toys™, Lincoln Logs™, Legos™, or other construction materials.

❑ Has an instinctive ability to find his/her way around unfamiliar territory.

Profile adapted from materials by Armstrong (1999, pp. 151-2) and Phipps (1997, pp.9-10).

SPATIAL INTELLIGENCE

Putting It into Action

With his strong sense of color, shape, and line, Stephon will respond to activities and materials that promote arts and crafts, construction, and anything visual. Adults can do the following to meet the needs of children like Stephon:

Promote arts and crafts:

● Give children chances for a variety of art projects (*painting, drawing, doodling, cartooning, sketching, fingerpainting*).
● Have a variety of paper available (*white paper, construction paper, sandpaper, newspaper, tissue paper, graph paper*).
● Provide a variety of writing, drawing, and painting materials (*pencils, pens, markers, paint brushes, paint, watercolors*).
● Give children materials that they can cut up for collages or other projects (*magazines, catalogs*).
● Offer a variety of materials for fastening things together (*glue, paste, tape, staplers, hole puncher, yarn, ribbon, stickers*).
● Offer art materials that allow for 3-dimensional creations (*clay, playdough, sculptures*).
● Give children recyclable materials or "junk" art with which to create (*milk cartons, boxes, lids, pie pans, straws, toothpicks*).
● Provide craft materials (*popsicle/craft sticks, sewing, weaving, plastic canvas and needles, beadwork, leatherwork*).

Promote construction:

● Provide a variety of block building materials (*wooden blocks, Tinker Toys™, Lincoln Logs™, Lego™s, erector sets*).
● Provide manipulatives that can be used with blocks (*dolls, action figures, vehicles, toy animals*).
● Have materials for construction projects (*wood, hammer, nails, screwdriver, screws, saw*).
● Allow children chances to take things apart and put them together (*old appliances with cords cut off, simple machines, jigsaw puzzles*).

(More activity and material ideas on next page.)

Promote the visual:

● Decorate space (*children's art, posters, bulletin boards, photographs*).
● Let children use visual materials (*camera, camcorder*).
● Use visual mediums in your environment (*movies, slides, computer graphics, multimedia*). *
● Provide children with highly-visual materials *(heavily-illustrated books, scrapbooks, photo albums, maps, graphs, charts, puzzles, mazes).*
● Label areas and materials with pictures and words.

* Movies and television should NOT be used on a regular basis. When used, it should be with parental permission (especially showing a movie) and be connected to other activities the children are doing (such as a theme).

Areas
Here's where Stephon, and other children like him, are most likely to find these materials and activities:

● art area
● building or block area
● manipulatives area
● construction area

● sewing area
● doll area
● computer area

BODY/KINESTHETIC INTELLIGENCE

Definition

Becca does not like to sit still. She wants to run and jump and move. People marvel at her natural talent for athletics; she seems capable of picking up any new sport with ease.

Even when she isn't hitting a ball or running across a field, she finds a way to put her body to work. She is a natural performer who relishes any chance to ham it up in skits, plays, or puppet shows. She also loves dancing, gymnastics, and cheerleading.

If she can't be outdoors or on a stage, she's likely to be elbow-deep in papier-maché, clay, or fingerpainting. If she can't find a messy enough project, she'll find other avenues to use her hands. She might tackle sewing, weaving, carving, carpentry, or model building.

Becca's body/kinesthetic intelligence gives her a wisdom of the body and an understanding and mastery of physical movement. She excels at any activity that lets her use either her gross motor or fine motor skills.

Body/kinesthetic intelligence is the ability to understand and master both gross motor and fine motor skills.

When she grows up, Becca might choose a profession that uses her gross motor skills (athlete, dancer, gymnast, cheerleader, actor). She could also lean on her fine motor abilities (craftsperson, sculptor, mechanic, or surgeon).

BODY/KINESTHETIC INTELLIGENCE

A Profile

How do you identify someone, either child or adult, as being strong in this intelligence? See if a majority of these characteristics fit. This person:

Profile adapted from materials by Armstrong (1999, p. 152) and Phipps (1997, p.10)

❏ Was an early crawler and/or walker.

❏ Has difficulty sitting for long periods of time.

❏ Learns best through hands-on activities.

❏ Is very physically active.

❏ Is well coordinated.

❏ Has an inkling for one or more sports.

❏ Has a "daredevil side" that likes thrilling, physical experiences.

❏ Loves being outdoors.

❏ Gets best ideas when out walking, jogging, or engaged in some other physical activity.

❏ Uses lots of hand gestures and body language in conversation.

❏ Likes performing (skits, plays, puppet shows, etc.).

❏ Is attracted to creative movement activities (dance, ballet, gymnastics, etc.).

❏ Enjoys messy, hands-on activities like papier-maché, clay, or fingerpainting.

❏ Works with his/her hands on concrete activities (sewing, weaving, carving, carpentry, or model building).

BODY/KINESTHETIC INTELLIGENCE

Putting It into Action

Because of her strong command of both gross and fine motor skills, Becca will respond to activities and materials that promote movement, creative dramatics and performance, and hands-on activities. Adults can do the following to meet the needs of children like Becca:

Promote activities that let children move:

● Provide materials for daily outdoor play (*balls, jump ropes, hula hoops*).
● Regularly offer active games and sports (*tag, softball, basketball*). *
● Find ways to do fun exercises for children (*a walking club, aerobics, fitness logs*).
● Let kids move from activity to activity or area to area at their own pace.
● Keep "sitting activities" to a minimum.
● Offer outdoor activities (*gardening, scavenger hunts*)
● Participate in field trips focused on movement-oriented activities (*sporting events, bowling, skating, swimming, parks, amusement parks*).

* Non-competitive games and sports are more developmentally appropriate for elementary-age children. For ideas, check out the book *Games, Games, Games: Creating Hundreds of Group Games and Sports* (in the Annotated Bibliography at the back of the book).

Promote creative dramatics and performance:

● Give children chances to role play and pretend (*house area, drama area, prop boxes*).
● Let children practice and perform various formats of creative expression (*dances, cheers, skits, plays, puppet shows, miming*).
● Attend field trips focused on performance (*plays, music, dance, puppetry*).

(*More activity and material ideas on next page.*)

Promote hands-on activities:

● Provide hands-on materials to children that they can touch and explore (*like science experiments and projects described in section on logical/mathematical intelligence*).

● Always have arts and crafts materials readily available for children (*see spatial intelligence*).

● Give children blocks and manipulatives that let them construct things (*see spatial intelligence*).

● Give children chances for construction and taking things apart (*see spatial intelligence*).

● Do cooking projects or other activities involving food.

● Provide materials for hobby-oriented pursuits (*model building, sewing, weaving*).

Areas

Here's where Becca, and other children like her, are most likely to find these materials and activities:

● outdoor area   ● house area

● gym   ● building or block area

● game area   ● art area

● drama area   ● music/performance area

MUSICAL INTELLIGENCE

Definition

 Mario is one of those "headphone singers." In the midst of whatever activity surrounds him, there he is, radio/CD player perched in his lap, headphones on, volume blaring. He sings, taps, hums, or snaps his fingers along with whatever tune is playing.

For Mario, anything has instrument potential. He was one of those tots who loved banging wooden spoons on metal pots. While most children grow out of that, he still does it. He is usually more interested in containers than their contents - he can't wait to dump them out, turn them upside down, and experiment with their percussive qualities.

Mario cooed to himself as an infant, enthralled with the sounds he discovered he could make. He is still captivated by whatever sounds he hears around him.

Because of his musical intelligence, Mario enjoys, creates, and performs music. He responds to rhythm, beat, tonal patterns, vibration, melody, harmony, movement, and anything else musical. One could say he marches to the beat of his own drum, but they'd be wrong. Mario will march to the beat of any drum.

> *Musical intelligence is the ability to relate to music through the enjoyment, creation, and performance of it.*

Mario could parlay his talents into any number of careers including singer, instrumentalist, conductor, composer, songwriter, jingle writer, music teacher, music critic, or musical stage performer.

MUSICAL INTELLIGENCE

A Profile

How do you identify someone, either child or adult, as being strong in this intelligence? See if a majority of these characteristics fit. This person:

Profile adapted from materials developed by Armstrong (1999, pp. 152-3) and Phipps (1997, p.10).

❏ Had an especially musical quality to babbling as an infant.

❏ Liked banging on toys, furniture, kitchen utensils, or other objects in a rhythmic way as a young child.

❏ Has a good ear for different kinds of nonverbal sounds (dogs barking, ice cream vendor, wind blowing, etc.).

❏ Frequently listens to favorite records, tapes, or compact discs.

❏ Often has a television jingle or other tune running through his/her mind.

❏ Knows the tunes to many different songs or musical pieces.

❏ Has a pleasant singing voice.

❏ Can tell when a musical note is off-key.

❏ Can hear a musical selection once or twice and be able to sing it back fairly accurately.

❏ Can easily keep time to a piece of music with a simple percussion instrument.

❏ Often makes tapping sounds or sings little melodies while working, studying, or learning something new.

❏ Likes to make up songs.

❏ Plays a musical instrument.

❏ Enjoys live musical performances.

MUSICAL INTELLIGENCE

Putting It into Action

With Mario's ear for all things musical, he will respond to activities and materials that promote the appreciation, performance, and creation of music. Adults can do the following to meet the needs of children like Mario:

Promote the appreciation of music:

● Give children chances to listen to music (*tape player, CD player, radio, headphones*).
● Play different kinds of music during certain parts of your program day.
● Provide children with a variety of recorded music and let them bring in their own. *
● Go on music-oriented field trips (*vocal music, instrumental music, concerts, orchestra, opera, musical theater*).
● Bring in guest speakers and performers (*music teacher, instrumental music teacher, singer, instrumental performer, musical theater performer*). Don't feel like you have to restrict yourself to professionals, either. Children could get a lot from seeing some kids from the local high school perform.

* This depends on two factors - first, your program's policy on children bringing things from home. Second, and more importantly, any music brought into the program should be approved first to assure children are not listening to music that other families might find objectionable.

Promote the performance of music:

● Sing songs as a group.
● Let children perform for the group (*songs, chants, raps*).
● Give children chances to play instruments for the group (*homemade or otherwise*).
● Allow for movement-oriented activities that children can perform for the group or others (*parades, dances, cheers, songs with gestures and movements*).

(*More activity and material ideas on next page.*)

Promote creation of music:

● Give children materials with which they can make their own instruments (*tubes, string, boxes, containers, lids*).

● Let children write their own lyrics or change words to existing songs.

● Encourage children to take familiar songs and reinvent them by singing them differently (*faster/slower, louder/softer, opera, rap*).

● Allow children time to develop and practice movement-oriented activities that they may later perform (*cheers, dances, parades*).

● Provide materials that allow children to compose their own music (*computer software; keyboard/synthesizer; percussive instruments like drums, maracas, and cymbals*).

● Give children ways to record or listen to their music (*tape recorder/player, microphone, karaoke*).

Areas

Here's where Mario, and other children like him, are most likely to find these materials and activities:

● music area

● sharing time

● dramatic play area

● performance area

● drama area

● prop boxes

● house area

● art area

INTERPERSONAL INTELLIGENCE

Definition

 Ian and Ida are those kinds of kids that are popular with everyone. They have natural leadership qualities and always know what is going on with everyone else.

Ian and Ida both love to do special jobs. They seem willing to do anything, but have their favorite jobs. Ian is a top-notch greeter. In his after-school program, he loves handing out notes to parents as they arrive to pick up their children.

Ida also loves any kind of job that lets her be a helper, but her favorite task is leading the group. Luckily she works in a program that gives children a lot of responsibility. Leading songs, making announcements, and explaining projects for the day might be restricted to the adults in some programs. Not in this one, however, where the talents of children like Ida and Ian have been put to work.

Both children are also remarkably in tune with others. They have been very successful peer helpers and conflict mediators. Ian and Ida are fair and compassionate in dealing with others; they both have a sense that the most important thing is to make sure that other people feel good.

> *Interpersonal intelligence is the ability to interact with people and understand them and their behaviors.*

Ian and Ida could end up being child care providers, teachers, counselors, managers, therapists, salespeople, religious leaders, politicians, trainers, or clinicians.

INTERPERSONAL INTELLIGENCE

A Profile

How do you identify someone, either child or adult, as being strong in this intelligence? See if a majority of these characteristics fit. This person:

❏ Warms up naturally to strangers.

❏ Is comfortable in the midst of a crowd.

❏ Has an easy time making friends.

❏ Has at least three close friends.

❏ Likes to get involved in social activity (work, school, church, organizations, community).

❏ Is a leader in clubs, groups, or other settings.

❏ Is in touch with whatever is going on around him/her socially (feuds, romances, gossip, etc.).

❏ Would rather go to a party than stay home alone.

❏ Easily feels compassion for individuals or groups of people and wants to help.

❏ Is frequently asked for advice or counsel from others.

❏ Is called on to help settle disputes.

❏ Goes to other people for help in working out problems.

❏ Likes to teach others.

❏ Prefers group sports like badminton, volleyball, or softball to solo sports like swimming or jogging.

❏ Would rather play an interactive game than video games or solitaire.

INTERPERSONAL INTELLIGENCE

Putting It into Action

Ian and Ida will respond to activities and materials that promote interaction, leadership, and understanding of others. Adults can do the following to meet the needs of children like Ian and Ida:

Promote interaction:

● Allow children free time to spend with friends. They need to be able to hang out, talk, socialize, and just be together.

● Have some kind of gathering on a daily basis. Use that time for sharing, discussions, and group activities.

● Give children opportunities for group projects where they can work with others instead of working alone.

● Incorporate children into planning. Give them chances to brainstorm ideas for activities and materials to use in your program.

● Develop clubs within your program, or make sure you support children's activities outside of your program by asking them about it and giving them chances to tell others. (*art club, sports clubs, chess club, walking club, nature club*) *

* If you do anything with clubs, make sure all children know they are allowed to join any club they wish. Do not make children feel excluded. That means you should also avoid designating some activities for boys only and others for girls only.

Promote leadership:

● Give children jobs (*greeter, circle time/gathering leader, clean-up helper, peer helper*).

● Allow children to help plan, lead, and evaluate activities.

● Bring in community leaders as guest speakers (*police, fire department, hospital, government, business leaders*).

● Encourage parents to come in and talk to children about their jobs or interests.

(*More activity and material ideas on next page.*)

Promote understanding of others:

● Give children opportunities to take on job responsibilities that let them help others (*tutor, peer helper, conflict mediator*).

● Allow children role-playing experiences, whether as a formal activity or something they can choose to do during free time (*dramatic play area, house area*).

● Encourage family involvement. Do activities that will promote a greater awareness of children's families (*family photos, maps showing where family members come from*).

● Provide activities and materials that promote awareness of other cultures. Study how people live in other countries.

Areas

Here's where Ian and Ida, and other children like them, are most likely to find these materials and activities:

● free time

● sharing time

● circle time/gathering

● dramatic play area

● house area

● doll area

● friendship area

● game area

INTRAPERSONAL INTELLIGENCE

Definition

 Ira gets described frequently with somewhat negative words like "loner" or "shy," but there are at least some who recognize his real strength — focus. Ira will take up a task and attack it with the fiercest of determination until it is finished. For example, if he starts an art project, he won't leave that area (if he has a choice) until the project is done.

Ira spends a lot of time alone, but not because he isn't comfortable with other kids. It's more because he's so comfortable with himself. Nearly every day out on the playground, he's off playing alone . He might bring a notebook outside and sit and write. He might sit the entire time and study an ant hill. Chances are, though, he'll do one activity, he'll do it by himself, and he'll be happy.

Ira doesn't give up on things easily. He's usually pretty positive and patient. If he's building with a set of blocks and they fall over, he'll just start building again without batting an eye. He'll keep at it until he accomplishes his goal.

Because of his intrapersonal intelligence, Ira has exceptional abilities at self awareness. He knows his strengths and limitations. He has a strong sense of focus and determination. He relishes time alone for self-reflection. No one knows quite how Ira ticks...but Ira sure knows how he ticks.

Intrapersonal intelligence is the ability to understand the self, including one's feelings and motivations.

As an adult, Ira might find himself in the same professions as Ian or Ida, but with a different focus. Because of his inward nature, Ira might be drawn toward teaching, psychology, counseling, therapy, or the clergy. He also might be a strong candidate for being a self-employed entrepreneur.

INTRAPERSONAL INTELLIGENCE

A Profile

Profile adapted from materials developed by Armstrong (1999, pp. 153-4) and Phipps (1997, p. 11).

How do you identify someone, either child or adult, as being strong in this intelligence? See if a majority of these characteristics fit. This person:

❏ Was aware of oneself as a separate identity fairly early in childhood.

❏ Is particularly self-reliant, strong-willed, and independent.

❏ Has a special hobby that he/she keeps to himself/herself.

❏ Has a special place to get away from everybody.

❏ Would rather spend a weekend alone in a cabin in the woods than be at a fancy resort with lots of people around.

❏ Keeps a personal journal to record events of his/her inner life.

❏ Spends a lot of time alone meditating, reflecting, or thinking about important life questions.

❏ Ponders life events (e.g., children will think about what they want to be when they grow up).

❏ Contemplates important life goals on a regular basis.

❏ Has a realistic view of personal strengths and weaknesses.

❏ Responds to setbacks with resilience.

❏ Has, as an adult, started own business or seriously considered starting one.

INTRAPERSONAL INTELLIGENCE

Putting It into Action

Ira needs time alone, time to reflect, and time to focus. He will respond to activities and materials that promote an option to being alone, self-reflection, and relaxation. Adults can do the following to meet the needs of children like Ira:

Promote the option of being alone:

● Children can choose if they wish to work with others or work alone. If a child needs time alone, there is space to allow for that (*alone area, quiet area*).

● It is acceptable for a child to choose to sit out and not participate in an activity (*or to do the activity in another way*). Sometimes the child may want to watch first.

● There are games that a child can play alone (*Solitaire, video games, computer games*). *

● There are activities that can be done alone (*computer, hobby materials*).

* Programs should be very cautious about using video games. First, they need to be appropriate. Second, they need to fit in with the program philosophy and not just be a tool to keep children busy. After all, this environment should be providing children something they cannot get elsewhere.

Promote self-reflection:

● Children have means of keeping track of their thoughts and projects (*journals, autobiographies, portfolios, folders, place for own belongings, scrapbooks*).

● Children have opportunities to assess themselves. This includes analysis of strengths, weaknesses, goals, and what they learned from an activity.

● Children are given time to think before being expected to speak or share.

(More activity and material ideas on next page.)

Promote relaxation:

● There is a balance of active and quiet activities.

● Children can choose which activities they want to do (at least part of the time).

● There is flexibility within activities to allow children to spend as much (or as little) time as they wish on it.

● There is time allowed after activities for children to reflect on what they have been doing. They do not have to immediately move into something else if they are not ready.

● Not only do children have "down" time in between activities, but there are chances throughout their program time to relax. A soft, cozy area in the room allows children a comfortable place for relaxation.

Areas

Here's where Ira, and other children like him, are most likely to find these materials and activities:

● free time
● alone area
● quiet area

● computer area
● reading area
● writing area

NATURALIST INTELLIGENCE

Definition

Mud puddles are magnets for Nayah. She is drawn to anything outdoorsy, especially the nooks and crannies where she might find some unusual critter. She is overjoyed to turn over a large rock and discover whatever lurks beneath.

If she isn't searching for critters, she's picking wild flowers, collecting rocks, or laying in the grass looking up at the clouds. She would live outdoors if she could.

When she is indoors, you can bet she'll be tending to some indoor plants or have her nose pressed up to an aquarium. She loves to make collections of rocks, leaves, and other items found in nature. She also loves using tools like magnifying glasses and microscopes to investigate her discoveries.

She also likes making weather charts and participating in recycling. She is the first one ready to go when the phrase "field trip" comes up. She relishes a chance to go the zoo or a park.

Nayah is very much in touch with the natural world. Her recognition, appreciation, and understanding of her environmental surroundings are key signs of her naturalist intelligence.

> *Naturalist intelligence is the ability to recognize, appreciate, and understand the natural world.*

Nayah has a number of possibilities for careers in her adult life. Among them are veterinarian, park ranger, nature guide, farmer, gardener, botanist, ecologist, geologist, zoologist, entomologist, zookeeper, or landscaper.

NATURALIST INTELLIGENCE

A Profile

Profile adapted from material created by Armstrong (1999, pp.227-8).

How do you identify someone, either child or adult, as being strong in this intelligence? See if a majority of these characteristics fit. This person:

❏ Spends a lot of time outdoors.

❏ Likes to study nature topics.

❏ Has animals around the house (more than just cats or dogs).

❏ Has/had an aquarium, terrarium, or ant farm.

❏ Participates in activities such as camping, hiking, back packing, fishing, birdwatching, or gardening.

❏ Likes taking nature walks.

❏ Takes trips to zoos, parks, campgrounds, hiking trails, nature museums, nurseries, aquariums, nature sanctuaries, etc.

❏ Watches nature shows on television.

❏ Is involved in an ecological organization (like Greenpeace).

❏ Enjoys capturing insects in bottles, putting leaves in scrapbooks, and collecting other items from nature.

❏ Loves watching birds/animals and following their habits (e.g., nesting, feeding) or finding out things about them.

❏ Is very aware of different kinds of animals, birds, fishes, trees, plants, rocks, or other items found in nature.

❏ Derives pleasure from looking at natural phenomena like clouds, trees, mountains, or other formations.

❏ Likes looking at animal tracks and guessing what kind of animals made them.

NATURALIST INTELLIGENCE

Putting It into Action

Nayah has a strong draw to the natural world and will respond to activities and materials that promote outdoor exploration. Adults can do the following to meet the needs of children like Nayah:

Promote outdoor exploration:

● Provide daily opportunity for outdoor play.
● Have outdoor activities that explore nature (*nature walks, gardening, scavenger hunts*).
● Give children materials with which to collect insects and other critters (*bug catchers, butterfly nets, ant farms*).

Promote the outdoors coming in:

● If possible, keep some kind of pet in your program (*fish, gerbils, hamsters*).
● With or without pets, have ways for children to bring outdoor critters inside (*such as the bug catchers and ant farms listed above*).
● Give children chances to make collections of natural materials (*rocks, leaves, insects*).
● Do nature-related art projects (*leaf rubbings, nature collages, rock painting, drawing nature scenes, etc.*).
● Provide toys that represent nature (*animals, insects, caves, forests*).
● Let children use materials that let them pretend they are doing an outdoor activity (*camping supplies, fishing, pretend boat*).
● Keep a texture tub in your space and supply it with natural materials (*pinecones, snow, water, gravel, twigs, leaves*).

(More activity and material ideas on next page.)

Promote exploration in general:

● Provide children with tools for exploration (*binoculars, microscopes, telescopes, and magnifying glasses*).
● Let children keep observation notebooks where they can keep track of what they see in nature (*animal habits, weather patterns, changing seasons*).
● Give children chances to take photographs of outdoor nature discoveries or indoor nature projects.
● Involve children in environmentally-oriented community service projects (*planting trees, recycling, trash pick-up*).

Areas

Here's where Nayah, and other children like her, are most likely to find these materials and activities:

● outdoor space
● nature area
● science area
● discovery area
● texture area

The Areas

NOTES

THE AREAS

The Basics

The first half of this book detailed the multiple intelligences in relation to the various ways children learn. The second half of the book advocates for a variety of interest centers in child-centered environments that satisfy learners of all intelligences.

Learning environments committed to allowing children a say in their own learning provide children with materials with which they can explore as they wish. These materials should be organized into areas based around various themes. Children should have access to areas that encourage:

- Creating (*art, sewing, model building areas*)
- Constructing (*carpentry, destruction, block areas*)
- Pretending and performing (*doll, house, drama, music areas*)
- Relaxing (*quiet/alone, collection, friendship areas*)
- Reading and writing (*reading, bookmaking, language areas*)
- Discovering (*science, nature, math, texture areas*)
- Playing games (*table game, floor game, outdoor areas*)

Space, materials, budgets, and number of children dictate how many areas can be established. However, in any learning environment, children should have access to at least one area in each of the above categories.

It should be noted that there is NOT an attempt to align areas with specific multiple intelligences. The idea is that children of different intelligences can work and play side by side in the same areas, despite using materials in potentially different ways. For example, Nayah might be in the art area making a nature collage while Becca plays with clay. Ira might be in this area working on a project by himself. Max might be using graph paper as Stephon paints a picture.

The benefit of this approach is that children learn from each other and learn new ways of doing things that they had not considered. They also gain a better sense of the interests and abilities of other children around them.

THE AREAS

Areas for Creating

Children need a place to express their imaginations and creativity through various mediums. Children can learn through visual arts (art area), craft-oriented endeavors (sewing area), or construction (carpentry area).

Because of his spatial intelligence, Stephon likes to come here to draw and paint.

The Art Area

The most obvious outlet for this kind of creative expression is through an art area. This area should have a variety of instruments and paper for drawing, painting, or writing. Consider:

Objects for drawing, painting, and writing:

pencils	thick markers	paint
erasers	thin markers	paint brushes
pens	crayons	chalk
pencil sharpeners		

Pencil and paper are all Luisa needs to tap into her linguistic intelligence by writing stories.

Materials for drawing, painting, and writing on:

construction paper	newsprint	wipe-off board
notebook paper	tissue paper	chalkboard
graph paper	scrap paper	easel

The art area should also provide children with three-dimensional materials and tools with which to create. Consider:

Materials with which to create:

magazines to cut up	streamers	yarn
cardboard scraps	lids	fabric/felt
cardboard boxes	caps	buttons
colored noodles	styrofoam	beads
pipe cleaners	beans	feathers
toothpicks	dried cereal	clay
googly eyes	popsicle sticks	string
toilet paper rolls	shells	paper bags
paper towel rolls	foam and wood shapes	

Tools for creating with:

scissors	clear tape	stamps
glue	stapler	stamp pads
colored glue	staples	stencils
glue sticks	hole punch	tools for dough
paste	rulers	paper clips
masking tape		

Due to her naturalist intelligence, Nayah likes to make nature collages in the art area.

As a way to explore his musical intelligence, Mario likes to make his own musical instruments.

Chances to work on hobby-oriented projects appeal to Ira's intrapersonal intelligence.

The Sewing Area

Children need opportunities for craft-oriented pursuits that can turn into life-long hobbies. A sewing area is one such approach. Consider:

Materials for sewing:

needles	yarn	buttons
thread	frames	hooks
plastic canvas	hoops	snaps
fabric	looms	beads
crochet hooks	pin cushion	ribbons
knitting needles	scissors	tape measure

The step-by-step sequence of model building appeals to Max's logical/ mathematical intelligence.

The Model Building Area

Model building is a great way for kids to get opportunities to delve into creation and develop a potentially life-long hobby as well. They are especially good for older children.

If you don't have dedicated space for your program or a good place to store and/or display models, you may have to be creative in developing this area. In any event, if this fits into your program's constraints, consider the following materials for this area:

Materials for model building:

snap-together model kits	model paints
glue-together model kits	paint brushes
model decals	table cloths
model glue	

Areas for Constructing

There is a fuzzy line between areas for creating and areas for constructing. The former focuses more on two-dimensional materials where children are less physically active. Areas dedicated to constructing provide children with more three-dimensional materials and space in which to use them.

Children's projects in these areas will frequently overlap but there should be separate areas devoted to creating and constructing (especially art and building areas). Children need both methods for expressing their visual and spatial abilities.

The Carpentry Area

Obviously tools require supervision, but that should not deter programs from finding ways to provide children with chances to use hammers and screwdrivers and such. Consider:

Materials for carpentry work:

soft wood (balsa, pine)	drills	cloths and rags
sandpaper	drill bits	string
hammer	wrench	wire
nails	vise	tape measure
screws	C-clamps	safety goggles
screwdriver	tape	workbench
	glue	broom, dustpan

The Destruction Area

Children like taking things apart as much as putting things together. Give children access to old appliances that they can take apart. Always remove cords and avoid radios and other appliances with warnings that opening them can result in electric shock.

Becca likes using her fine motor skills in any kind of construction project because it lets her explore her body/kinesthetic intelligence.

Because of his logical/ mathematical intelligence, Max loves to explore how things work by putting them together and taking them apart.

Stephon loves to use his spatial intelligence skills in building villages and streets.

Ian and Ida focus on their interpersonal intelligence through their play that revolves around the interactions of the people within the communities that they construct.

The Building (or Block) Area

Children need access to blocks and manipulatives that let them create roads, cities, and houses. Such materials give them a very different spatial awareness than what they experience through arts and crafts. Consider the following materials:

Building materials:

wooden blocks	Legos™	roads
foam blocks	Lincoln Logs™	boards

Recyclable materials:

large boxes	plastic containers	toilet paper rolls
small boxes	styrofoam	paper towel rolls

Manipulatives to use with creations:

toy people	toy animals	planes
action figures	trucks and cars	boats

Materials for creating life-size structures:

tents	chairs	tape
sheets	string	rugs

Areas for Pretending and Performing

Children also express themselves through pretending and performing.

The Doll Area

Dolls are a wonderful means to allow children to pretend to be someone else. They can interact with the dolls or use them to represent various aspects of themselves or other people. Either way, children gain valuable experience with pretending and practicing at interactions with others. Consider the following materials:

baby dolls	doll house	Barbies/other dolls
baby doll clothes	doll house people	clothes for dolls
crib/bed	doll house furniture	blankets
		accessories

Due to his intrapersonal intelligence, Ira likes to watch others perform and sometimes engages in role play as a way of exploring various sides of himself.

The House Area

A house area allows children to role play various characters and scenes, as well as reflect on the interactions that they see in the people around them. Consider the following materials:

Kitchen supplies:

table	empty food cartons	toy sink
dishes	tins and jars	toy stove
silverware	play food	toy fridge
cups	aprons	
place mats	old household appliances (with cords cut off)	

Let Mario's musical intelligence loose with the kitchen supplies and he's bound to put together a one-man band with spoons and pots and pans.

Other household materials:

telephones	rocking chair	couch

Any of the pretending and performing areas appeal to Ian and Ida's interpersonal intelligence since they both love interacting with other people and engaging in role play.

The Drama Area

A drama area can be an extension of the house area. It gives children opportunities for role play and interaction that may turn into performances. Consider dress-up clothes and objects for creating environments:

Materials for dressing up:

dresses	ties	jackets
skirts	scarves	raincoats
shirts	fake fur	winter coats
pants	belts	capes
belts	suspenders	graduation gowns
shoes	tutus	full length mirror
boots	dance shoes	

Materials with which to accessorize:

jewelry	purses	umbrellas
eyeglass frames	handbags	
sunglasses	brief cases	

Stephon loves to use his own handmade puppets, costumes, and masks to explore his spatial intelligence.

Materials with which to create environments:

curtains	sheets	puppets
streamers	tents	lace
cardboard	costumes	masks
stage (real or created)		

Multiple Intelligences & After-School Environments

Prop Boxes

Prop boxes can be part of a drama or house area or stand alone. The concept is to group materials around a certain theme. These boxes serve as wonderful tools for role playing or performance. Consider these possible themes:

travel agency	gas station	office
school	auto mechanic	hair stylist
veterinarian	magic show	beach
TV station	mall/store	fitness/health club
comedy club	restaurant	

Because of her body/ kinesthetic intelligence, Becca relishes opportunities for performance and play that let her use her whole body.

The Music Area

This is an area for listening, dancing, singing, and cheerleading. Children with interest in music, creative movement, and performance may all be drawn to this area. Consider:

Equipment for listening to music:

CDs/tapes of music	tape player	radio
CD player	headphones	

Equipment for making music:

bells	banjo	xylophone
drums	guitar	maracas
tambourines	rattles	other instruments
homemade instruments		

Equipment for recording music:

song book	tape recorder
microphone	blank tapes

Mario's musical intelligences thrives in this area where he can perform and create his own music.

Areas for Relaxing

The areas for relaxing can provide materials that will interest many of the children. That's because the focus of this area is more on providing children with chances to work alone or in small groups and is less focused on the actual materials.

The Quiet/Alone Area

As a result of his intrapersonal intelligence, Ira likes a place where he can work, play, and think by himself.

This gives kids a place to wind down and be by themselves. This area may have materials that you could find in other areas (such as reading and writing materials from the language area, prisms and kaleidoscopes from the science/math area, the sewing area, etc.), but you can also add individual games, puzzles, and activities to this area. Possibilities include:

puzzles	plants	pillows
beads	photo albums	bean bags
string for beads	word games	

The Collection Area

Sorting and classifying objects in collections appeals to Max's logical/mathematical intelligence.

Children can have opportunities to work on and create collections of various items through materials in the quiet/alone area or in an area devoted just to collections. Possible materials include:

bottle caps	sports cards	comics
coins	other trading cards	insects
stickers	rocks	marbles
decals	stamps	shells
postcards	buttons	patches

The Friendship Area

It is important that every program have a place for children to be alone (either by their choice or an adult's request). However, at times this same area could be available to small groups of children (two or three) that want to spend quiet time with friends. If you have space, try to create both an alone area and a friendship area. Materials may be very similar, but the expectations of the areas would be that the alone area is for only one person at a time and the friendship area is limited to two or three.

Ian and Ida's interpersonal intelligence draws them to this area where they can talk and share with friends.

The collection area, on the previous page, is a great place for Nayah to explore her naturalist intelligence by creating collections of natural materials such as rocks, leaves, and shells.

Due to her linguistic nature, Luisa loves to spend time reading books.

Areas for Reading and Writing

Reading and writing areas should give children opportunities to experience language in different ways than the traditional classroom setting. Areas should be devoted to children's interests and abilities.

The Reading Area

Books and other reading materials are an integral part of any learning environment. In addition, the space should be comfortable and inviting. Consider including:

fiction books	reference books	magazines
library books	newspapers	comic books
comfortable reading space		

Stephon's spatial intelligence draws him to any area where he can create things. He loves to write and illustrate his own books.

The Bookmaking Area

Either along with the reading area or separate from it, there should also be an area devoted to writing. Consider including the following in a bookmaking area:

computer	hole punch	stamps
pencils	stapler	stamp pad
pens	yarn	stickers
markers	scissors	chalk board
notebook paper	tape	chalk
construction paper	notebooks	stationery
comfortable writing space		

The Language Area

This area could encompass both the reading and bookmaking areas, but could also include other language-oriented activities and materials such as:

crossword puzzles	sign language book/poster
word searches	alphabet poster
calendar	journal

The Homework Area

This gives kids a place to work on homework if they choose. This area can be set up in conjunction with the language area to allow children access to reading and writing materials that they might need. Consider materials from the area focused on discovering that would also aid kids in working on homework.

An area devoted to getting work done is a blessing for someone like Ira, who is strong in intrapersonal intelligence.

Here's a thought - it might be separate from the homework area, but children like Mario might like time to practice a musical instrument.

Areas for Discovering

Children need to experiment and investigate and make new discoveries. This can be done through several means.

The Science Area

This is a place that provides children with tools for investigating and studying. Consider:

Tools for discovering and experimenting:

magnifying glasses	timers	rainsticks
microscopes	straws	maps
unbreakable mirrors	prisms	globes
thermometer	batteries	flashlight
eye droppers	kaleidoscopes	magnets
weather charts	tornado in a bottle	

The Nature Area

Children can bring the outdoors inside to study. Consider:

terrarium	bugs/bug catcher	plants
aquarium	ant farm	gardening tools

The Texture Area

A texture area lets children use their sense of touch to experiment with different materials. Consider these tools:

cups	squeeze bottles	beach shovel
containers	hoses	sand toys
funnels	pitchers	buckets
eye droppers	sponges	boats
sifters	mops	spoons

Luisa likes to record her observations in writing, a skill which focuses on her linguistic intelligence.

Nayah's naturalist intelligence thrives in the science area where she can study various items from nature.

The Texture Area, continued

All the tools for pouring and measuring are meaningless without stuff to pour and measure! Consider these textures:

water	grass	paper confetti
sand	seeds	twigs and branches
dirt	feathers	pine cones
shells	wood chips	soap flakes
bark	sawdust	papier-maché
leaves	beads	shaving cream
clay	buttons	beans
plaster	oatmeal	macaroni
rocks and pebbles	rice	gelatin
styrofoam peanuts		

Because she's very body/kinesthetic, Becca loves the hands-on experience of manipulating various textures.

The Math Area

This could be its own area, but is more likely to be combined with the Science Area (possibly called the Discovery Area). Consider the following materials to meet the needs of children interested in numbers:

pencils/pens	dominoes	tape measure
pencil sharpener	calculator	scales
note paper	compass	weights
graph paper	abacas	stencils of shapes
strategy games	yardstick	ruler
logic puzzles		
objects for counting/sorting		

Any of the discovery areas intrigue Max's logical/mathematical intelligence since he gets to focus on scientific observation and numbers.

Areas for Playing Games

Games can provide children with very different experiences. A card game may be more about sitting and chatting with friends; a softball game might be about exerting energy. Games can be indoors or out, active or calm. Here are a few ideas:

The Table Game Area

Table games can hit many different interests. Games can vary from strategy or matching games to language-oriented or art-oriented games (like Pictionary™):

Thanks to their interpersonal intelligence, Ian and Ida love to socialize while playing games with friends.

Board games:

checkers	Monopoly™	Chutes and Ladders™
chess	Sorry™	backgammon
Connect 4™	Candyland™	trivia games
dominoes	Scrabble™	

Card games:

playing cards	Skip-Bo™	memory game
Uno™	Old Maid	

Luisa loves to use her linguistic intelligence in writing rules for games.

Materials for making up games:

markers	pencils	extra dice
pens	ruler	extra playing pieces
cardboard	compass	
stencils	business cards (to make cards)	
containers for games/materials		

The Floor Game Area

Of course, there are some games that work better on the floor. Here are a few:

> Twister™   marbles
>
> pickup sticks   jacks

The Outdoor Area

Children also need time to be outside to do more active games. Here's some equipment that you can provide:

Balls:

> utility balls   soccer ball   baseball
>
> kickball   basketball   tennis balls
>
> football   volleyball   wiffle balls

As a result of her naturalist intelligence, Nayah relishes any opportunity to be outdoors.

Sports equipment:

> bats   rackets   hockey sticks
>
> gloves   portable goal/net   bases
>
> cones (for boundaries)   air pump

Small group games and activities:

> jump ropes   hopscotch   badminton
>
> frisbees   horseshoes   ring toss

Becca loves games and sports because it gives her the means to use her body/kinesthetic intelligence.

Individual games and activities:

> hula hoops   batons   kites
>
> yo-yo's   bubbles

Final Thoughts

Except for the focus on the outdoors as a place for playing games, there has been no mention of activities and materials for outside. Just about anything you can play with inside can become an outside toy as well. Stay away from items with multiple pieces, like board games, or paper that can get blown away (card games, art supplies), but consider materials from your block, drama, house, and science areas. Here are some materials designed for outdoor play:

Building and creating:

climbing equipment	sand toys
sidewalk chalk	crates
cardboard for hill sliding	large blocks
cardboard for hideouts	cartons
sheets for forts/hideouts	

Getting around:

stilts	scooters	carts
pogo sticks	wagons	

Seasonal:

water play - hoses, sprinklers, wading pools, buckets, bottles, balloons
snow play - shovels, sleds, saucers
gardening - seeds, plants, containers, watering can, tools

At the onset of this section, you were encouraged to develop areas based around seven themes:

- Creating
- Constructing
- Pretending and performing
- Relaxing
- Reading and writing
- Discovering
- Playing games

It can't be emphasized enough that a program certainly doesn't need every single area represented here. However, a good learning environment needs at least one area for each of the seven themes. In some cases, you may combine some of the areas mentioned (like creating a discovery area with recommended materials from the science, math, and texture areas).

You might also rotate some areas. Just make sure that you have consistent areas as well. Try not to have more than one or two "temporary" areas at a time. Children need to know that there are reliable areas and materials that will always be there.

If you are committed to children learning and having fun simultaneously, then this approach should help immensely. By understanding the varied ways in which children learn and creating areas that focus on children's different interests, then you can have the best of both worlds - productive learning that is also fun. On that note, you have hopefully learned something from this book and had fun as well.

NOTES

ANNOTATED BIBLIOGRAPHY

Multiple Intelligences Resources

Armstrong, T. (1999). *7 kinds of smart*. New York, NY: New American Library.

> This book covers the seven originally identified intelligences plus the two that have been explored since then. Easy-to-use descriptions, inventories, and suggestions for improving intelligences make this book a must-have.

Armstrong, T. (1999). *Multiple intelligences in the classroom*. Alexandria, VA: Association for Supervision and Curriculum Development.

> This book offers inventories for assessing children's MI's, discusses how to develop curriculum around MI's, and discusses how MI relates to teaching strategies, classroom management and assessment.

Armstrong, T. (2000). *Multiple intelligences*. Retrieved October 2000 from the Thomas Armstrong web site on the World Wide Web: http://www.thomasarmstrong.com/multiple_intelligences.htm

> Succinct definitions of the multiple intelligences parallel Armstrong's work in the books already cited.

Campbell, B. (1999). "Multiplying Intelligence in the Classroom." New Horizons for Learning On The Beam, Vol. IX No. 2 Winter 1989 p.7:167. Retrieved October 2000 from the New Horizons for Learning web site on the World Wide Web: http://www. newhorizons.org/art_ miclsrm.html

> Campbell details how he developed centers around each of the intelligences and rotated his third grade students through them on a daily basis.

Gardner, H. (1993). *Frames of mind: The theory of multiple intelligences*. New York, NY: Basic Books.

> This is the first. Gardner's first edition of this book, published in 1983, introduced the world to multiple intelligences. In a more scientific approach than his followers, Gardner dissects the definition of intelligence and presents his case as to why there are multiple intelligences.

Gardner, H. (1993). *Multiple intelligences: The theory in practice*. New York, NY: Basic Books.

> This reader was compiled to celebrate the ten years that passed since Gardner first proposed the theory of MI. This compilation of papers and speeches that he did during that time is much more user-friendly than his first book and explores how MI can be used in teaching.

Lazear, D. (1998). *Multiple intelligences overview: 8 ways of knowing*. Retrieved October 2000 from the Oak Tree Centre web site on the World Wide Web: http://www.oaktreecentre.com/Visual/spatial.htm

> This web page offers quick, two-line explanations of the eight intelligences.

Phipps, P. (1997). *Multiple intelligences in the early childhood classroom*. Columbus, OH: SRA/McGraw-Hill.

> This book focuses on the original seven intelligences and how to identify them in children and develop program space, materials, discipline methods, and assessment to their particular intelligences.

Phipps, P. (1998). *Chapter 6: Tips for success*. Retrieved October 2000 from the California Collaborative After-School/School-Age Project web site on the World Wide Web: http://www.gse.uci.edu/schoolage/studChapter6.html

> This web page addresses how children learn by focusing on development areas and the multiple intelligences. Each intelligence is accompanied by a chart that summarizes it, suggests what children of this intelligence like, and what you can try with these children.

Rheault, K. (No copyright year cited). *Using multiple intelligences to enhance learning*. Retrieved October 2000 from the World Wide Web: http://members.tripod.com/~RheaultK/

> Rheault offers a quiz for teachers to determine if MI is right for their classrooms and then details a four-step process for integrating MI in the classroom. She also describes potential activity interests for children of each intelligence.

Whitaker, David L. *Games, games, games: Creating hundreds of group games & sports*. 1996. Nashville: School-Age NOTES.

> A collection of easy group games, along with ideas and insights on how to create new games. See reference on page 31.